# Between Two Covers
## Poems Given to Me by God

by

Terry Billetter

The contents of this work including, but not limited to, the accuracy of events, people, and places depicted; opinions expressed; permission to use previously published materials included; and any advice given or actions advocated are solely the responsibility of the author, who assumes all liability for said work and indemnifies the publisher against any claims stemming from publication of the work.

All Rights Reserved
Copyright © 2014 by Terry Billetter

No part of this book may be reproduced or transmitted, downloaded, distributed, reverse engineered, or stored in or introduced into any information storage and retrieval system, in any form or by any means, including photocopying and recording, whether electronic or mechanical, now known or hereinafter invented without permission in writing from the publisher.

Dorrance Publishing Co
701 Smithfield Street
Pittsburgh, PA 15222
Visit our website at *www.dorrancebookstore.com*

ISBN: 978-1-4349-6968-2
eISBN: 978-1-4349-6888-3

# DEDICATION

I dedicate this book of poems to the Author and Overseer of all the words contained herein. I acknowledge God as the One and Only Almighty, divine, true and sacred, holy Creator of the Universe. Although my name appears on this book, I am just His humble servant, whom He used to write down these beautiful poems. Praise to the Lord forever!

Psalm 51:15
*O Lord, open my lips, that my mouth may declare Thy praise.*

# ACKNOWLEDGEMENT

I would like to give special thanks to my precious friend, Marie Thomas, who is responsible for editing these poems and whose guidance and tremendous help made this book possible.

# INTRODUCTION

There are times when I climb into my bed, cozy and comfortable, settling down under the covers, thanking and praising God for all His blessings, and somewhere in my thoughts, accompanied by a restlessness, a beautiful line of words suddenly comes to my mind—and then another and another and I know that one of God's poems is in the making.

It is a rather strange process because it doesn't always flow easily, but I know better than to ignore it, or it will not be given to me again, and the restlessness will not cease. That's how I write the poems that you are about to read in this book. Know that they come from God Himself.

If I were to take a pen in hand, intending to write on my own, it would not be worth reading. When I first read the poem, it doesn't always sound that great, but when I wake up the next morning and read it, or wait to read it several days later, I'm amazed and surprised at how beautiful it is.

Another unusual thing about these poems is that once I write them down, I cannot remember the words He gave me unless I read them again. To Him I give all the glory, honor, and praise He deserves for these beautiful poems that He has given to me.

Terry Billetter

# BETWEEN TWO COVERS
### August 2, 2006

*After completing the Study of Genesis in a Bible Study at the end of May in 2006, I was inspired to write this poem when thinking late one night about God's beautiful relationship with Abraham.*

Where do we find You, oh, sweet Lord?
    how do we know Your ways?
We look between two covers,
    back to the Ancient of Days.

You revealed Yourself to the prophets,
    who foretold of things to come,
Through 66 chapters and 888 pages,
    from Genesis to Revelation.

Though sad and disappointed
    after the fall of man,
In Your infinite wisdom and mercy,
    salvation was in Your plan.

You came to our rescue
    each time we fell into sin,
Provided we repented
    and returned to You again.

Your love for us is endless,
    these pages tell the story,
Of Your mercy and forgiveness,
    rich and full of Your glory.

It's all between two covers,
    the intimacy You desire with us,
As the center of all we do throughout the day,
    and through the evening's hush.

# ON THIS SIDE OF YOU
January 1, 2005


On this side of You much is unknown
   on this side of You we are here, but not home.

We live in the faith of what we can't see
   in the future that one day we know will be.

Your promise of peace, Your promise of hope,
   gives us courage each day to live and to cope.

On this side of You, You help us each day,
   although we can't see You, You show us the way.

We need only believe that Your way is best,
   to remain in Your presence where You give us rest.

And when you call us to You, on the other side,
   all will be known, as You carry us home.

# THE WORD OF GOD
November 2, 2005

Your words shine like gold, Your thoughts gleam like silver,
    Your holiness pure like diamonds, the sum of all treasure incalculable.

Your truth in my mind, Your love in my heart,
    Your imprint on my soul – indelible.

Your wisdom is brilliant as the fire of a million suns,
    and when my eyes are opened to it, we are One.

Your tenderness and caring ways are sure,
    they touch my mind, heart, and soul, where they endure.

Your protection from evil, by the sword of the Spirit,
    is my safe haven as I dwell within it.

# THOUGHTS OF YOU
## April 16, 2005

I go to sleep with You each night
    taking You into my heart and mind,
While You carry me safely to the dawn,
    keeping me safe from every harm.

You wake me every morning
    from the depths of unconsciousness
Into a brand new day,
    from a sweet, refreshing rest.

To praise You from a humble heart
    with a love deep in my soul,
A love that is not only new each day
    but a love that is very old.

For You loved me before the Creation of time
    and You knew me way back then.
And You gave me the love that is only Yours.
    so I could love You back again.

# GO TO WHERE GOD IS
April 29, 2006

Go to where God is—
    get lost in His presence.
Succumb to His peacefulness,
    wrap yourself in His essence.

His Spirit is a mystery
    yet clearly revealed,
To the faithful believer
    to the unbeliever concealed.

His word is the truth,
    our guide in all things.
With blessings and love
    our lives He brings.

Ponder His teachings,
    unwrap them with care,
Digest every morsel
    of wisdom that's there.

He is God Almighty,
    Creator of the universe,
Dividing earth and sky,
    setting the planets on course.

Praise Him, love Him
    with all your spirit, soul, and heart,
Revere Him, endear Him
    never let His Word depart.

# WORTHY
June 12, 2006

Worthy is the Son of God
    worthy is the Lamb,
Who shed His blood at Calvary
    to fulfill His Father's plan.

He went to the Cross willingly
    He exercised free will,
Force was not a factor,
    He willingly paid our bill.

He took all our sin upon Himself,
    as He hung there shamed and disgraced,
Was abandoned and separated from God,
    all this for the human race.

Victory was sweet at Resurrection,
    worthy is the Lamb!
Who paid with His blood for our salvation,
    His death, our reconnection, with God's perfect master plan.

Unworthy of Your forgiveness,
    unworthy of Your grace,
Unworthy of Your love
    for this sinful human race.

Worthy through Your forgiveness,
    worthy through Your grace,
Worthy through the Resurrection
    because Christ took our place.

# SUBMISSION
### February 4, 2008

I submit myself to you, Lord, morning, noon, and night
    and ask for Your protection
With Your omnipotent might.

The enemy prowls around me, looking for a way of attack,
    but I know I hold the power through Your precious Word
To keep him at bay and hold him back.

He fears Your Word and has to flee; he has no power against it
    he retreats in submission—battle won,
To return to his home in the pit.

# YOUR LOVE
### February 25, 2009

Your love for me is endless, eternal, and true,
    You're as faithful to me
As you were to the prophets
    when they were obedient to You.

You bring me through the desert,
    and each trial, one by one,
When I rely on You, Your Holy Spirit
    and Your beautiful, precious Son.

I know that You protect me
    as I travel through each day,
I'll never know how,
    I'll never know Your Ways.

Your Word says Your Ways are
    higher than ours
Ways we cannot understand
    in this day and hour.

I know You're ever-present
    in all I think and do,
That's why I pray my life's been pleasing
    when I stand in front of You.

# HOLY SPIRIT
April 9, 2003

Oh, Holy Spirit,
    oh, Joy of mine,
Dear Holy Spirit,
    true love divine.

Oh, holy night,
    oh, joyful night
Your Spirit fills me
    with deep delight.

Your Spirit flows through me
    like clear bubbling springs,
That open my eyes
    to so many things.

I have seen Your power
    I have felt Your comfort,
Awake in the day,
    and before deep slumber.

# ENDLESS LOVE
### September 13, 2003

His love for us is endless
    far out beyond the blue,
It's up and down and all around
    and it's deep within us, too.

He holds you tight within His hand
    so you would not be lost.
He held you close into His heart
    and took you to the Cross.

We didn't suffer with Him that day,
    He did that all alone.
It was His blood – His sweat – His agony,
    so we could share His throne.

## YOU MAKE ME WHOLE
### February 3, 2003

You are the tingling in my brain.
    You are the blood-rush through my veins.
You are the pounding in my heart, Your energy imparts.

You are the pulsing of my soul.
    You are my brave and courage bold.
It is You that makes me whole – my Lord.

You are my calming shade of green,
    quiet presence – cool and clean.
Rest and solitude serene – my Lord.

## SURROUNDED BY YOU
### Summer 2004

Wherever I am
    in the space that I'm in,
I'm surrounded by you, Lord,
    You're the sweetness within.

You're here in the morning
    from sunrise to sunset,
And all through the night
    while You give me Your rest.

Your silence is golden,
    Your presence is dear,
I treasure Your wisdom,
    with each passing year.

Your love takes my spirit
    far beyond this earth,
To the place where I knew You
    long before my birth.

# THE BLUEPRINT AND THE PLAN
### August 25, 2001

You made the blueprint.
    You know the plan.
And all that we do
    is guided by Your Hand.

The print unfolds
    as we travel our way.
When we soon learn to realize
    You are our mainstay.

## AT THE END
### August 25, 2001

Time is up – it's over,
    to seek Him and believe Him
To claim Him as Your Savior
    at the curtain's last call.

If you haven't found Him
    you'll be left out in the cold,
Where Satan will be waiting
    to swallow you whole.

He gave you a whole lifetime
    to search and to pray,
Wake up and find Him,
    right now – this minute – today.

# UNCHANGING GOD
October 15, 2008

Everyone has a story
    each with a different name,
But the God who answers all prayers
    always remains the same.

Some may wait just a little while;
    others a much longer time.
He'll always reward your test of patience,
    as He works His Master Design.

Don't let the tears of sorrow
    steal your joy away
For when His answered prayer comes along
    it will be a most glorious day!

# THOUGHTS OF YOU
### February 22, 2008

Too busy thinking thoughts of You
    to be bothered by worrisome things.
As I meditate on Your Word, Lord,
    I'm filled with the hope and confidence it brings.

By being in Your Presence
    my spirit soars so high
It climbs up to the heaven
    to where my soul does fly.

Where I experience
    Your indescribable joy
There we are together
    You and I.

# IN YOUR PRESENCE
## February 2, 2009

I feel the best when I'm in Your Presence,
    knowing we're together.
Confident that inside of me
    You have taken up residence.

I burst with praise as I think of Your goodness,
    when I speak to others
To which I am always ready
    to give witness.

These moments of praise overflow my spirit
    and bring gratitude to my heart.
Happiness and peace surround me
    as all other thoughts depart.

It's a total concentration on You, Lord,
    within which I dwell;
So beautiful, peaceful, and loving,
    and everyone I feel I must tell.

True, it's impossible to describe.
    because it's the Holy Spirit,
Communicating with my spirit
    with words and thoughts alive.

The only way you can experience this
    is communicating with God on your own,
By being in a silent place –
    you with Him alone.

# THE BIBLE
February 18, 2008

You may think that the words that lie on His pages
    have no power or might.
But trust me, I know, they do God's holy battle
    as against the enemy they fight.

The Word of God is a mighty weapon
    to thwart all enemy attacks,
When confronted with God's Word, Satan's strategy dissolves,
    and the Word forces him to stand back.

Read them aloud, and feel their power
    as your confidence swells,
For the Father, the Son, and the Holy Spirit
    within each one of them dwells.

When fear or distress should fill your mind,
    God's Word will cut like a sword.
Through the problems you face,
    so you can triumphantly leave them behind.

# YOUR PRESENCE
### September 3, 2008

It's Your Presence, not the words I speak
    to describe You that makes You real,
It's what I sense,
    and what I feel.

Words cannot penetrate the realm
    of where You are;
You're here and there – everywhere,
    yet far.

Wonderful books are written about You,
    beautiful hymns and songs are sung in praise.
Yet nothing begins to scratch the surface
    of Your beautiful and complex ways.

But our spirit knows much better
    what the mind can't comprehend,
It's a sacred, holy life united
    with God, in that place that has no end.

# ULTIMATE SACRIFICE
### September 22, 2008

Your death and resurrection are always with me
    never far from thought or mind.
Your suffering and loneliness – Your walk to the Cross
    not just at Easter time.

I ponder this and ask myself
    how did You stand the pain,
Even knowing the end result
    and what there was to gain?

The motivating force of Your amazing love
    that got You through it all,
Is eternal salvation for each of us –
    God's salvation for us all.

# THE GOOD BOOK
### March 14, 2007

Your Word is old
    Your Word is new
It's there for us
    to always turn to.

No matter what situations
    life brings your way,
Open your Bible
    right now – today.

God's direction is there
    His guidance is clear,
As you read His words
    that keep Him near.

## PERFECTION
May 18, 2007

Flawless and perfect
    that is what You are,
Mighty and powerful
    both near and far.

Master Designer
    of the whole universe,
Who positioned the planets
    and the stars dispersed.

Every intricate calculation
    came from You,
Your works are matchless
    in all that You do.

# THE TESTING GROUND
October 22, 2008

I've been on this testing ground before, Lord,
    where it looks like You haven't answered my prayers.
But I know better than to trust my physical senses—
    I know not to even dare.

I've learned to ignore words
    that I hear,
For they come not from You
    if they bring doubt or fear.

The enemy tries to defeat and discourage
    when You, Lord,
With the power of Your Word,
    in truth You encourage.

So trust not your senses
    and emotions so fleeting,
They will cause you to doubt
    your faith and believing.

Hold on to the promises
    of God's Holy Word.
They are love and goodness
    and answered prayers assured.

## JOY IN THE LORD
### June 6, 2004

Lord, the joy of You
    sings sweetly in my soul,
In mind, and in body
    that makes me feel whole.

You are the music that has not yet been written,
    the lyrics of the past.
You're the notes and rhythms, songs and symphonies
    that all throughout time will last.

# EXISTENCE OF GOD
October 22, 2004

Lord, You are my truest love,
    my greatest anticipation.
Yet there are those who deny You
    and Your exquisite creation.

How can they believe that You don't exist,
    when Your Presence is everywhere?
When the red in the tulip, the green in the grass
    and the blue of the sky persists?

How can they look at a newborn baby
    and not see Your love in its face?
How can they touch its petal-soft skin
    and not sense Your sweet, gentle grace?

I'm thankful my eyes are wide open,
    my heart and mind as well.
To receive Your love and wisdom
    and Your goodness for me to tell.

## MY LOVE FOR YOU, LORD
March 21, 2006

Each day I offer my life to You, Lord,
    right to Your heart it goes.
It's my way of expressing my deep love for You
    from my head down to my toes.

You live in every fiber, ooze out of every pore,
    reading Your beautiful Word makes me
Want to stay close to You,
    even that much more.

I praise You in song,
    and I speak of You in word
To those whom I meet
    so I will be heard.

It excites me to speak
    of Your mercy and grace
That You have bestowed
    on the whole human race.

Your constant concern
    and Your love for mankind,
Goes beyond comprehension
    in the human mind.

Your love song, oh Lord,
    is a dance through Your Word
That sings in the pages
    of Holy Scripture.

It jumps off Bible pages
    straight into my heart,
Making me thankful
    that I'm one of Your creatures.

You're the excitement in my spirit
   the contentment in my mind.
You're the comfort in my soul
   to be with forever, and for all time.

# BREATH OF LIFE
### May 20, 2002

You gave me breath, Lord, so I could live,
    You gave me love,
So I could give.

You gave me Your Word for me to read,
    You gave me Your Word
So it could be heard.

Your Spirit came into my parts
    to join with my spirit,
Mind and heart.

My soul is filled with songs of praise,
    that I will sing to You
All the rest of my days.

# MOTIVATION
### July 17, 2006

I'm motivated by Your Words
    that take me down a path
Expressing my emotions
    in thoughts I try to grasp.

Sometimes they come to me quickly,
    sometimes in a gentle flow,
But whatever method You choose, Lord,
    they come from You, I know.

# BIBLE STUDY
October 9, 2006

As we unravel Your Word in study
    a little more of You is revealed,
Taking us to another level
    that was previously concealed.

Your Word, so full of wisdom, that we try
    to discern, deep, and yet so simple
Testifies to Your love
    for which we all yearn.

We peel off the outer layers
    until we reach the core,
Only to discover
    there's yet even more!

# SILENCE
December 18, 2006

I find You in silence
    in the absence of noise,
Your presence surrounds me
    always well poised.

You lift me upward
    where all is serene
Feeling peaceful and calm
    drifting into a dream.

# HEAVEN
March 5, 2007

There is nothing in Heaven unhappy,
    sadness and sorrow do not exist.
We travel this journey onward
    that's why in this life we persist.

To live in God's presence forever, reward
    for our struggle and pain, no memory of heartaches – never!
We'll be given the crown of the kingdom
    that all heaven will Jesus acclaim!

# YOUR DECISION
## March 11, 2007

You decide, Holy Spirit, when to give me
    the words that I write,
You decide what words to give me
    very late at night.

Sometimes You do all the work
    as the words flow through me that rhyme,
Other times You are silent and
    we are together in sacred time.

# JESUS
### September 19, 2007

Your name, dear Jesus, is matchless
    it is You that I adore.
With each passing day
    I grow to love You even more.

Your love is sweet and tender, Your justice
    always fair, to Your mercy and compassion,
None other can compare.
    A match to Your perfection does not exist anywhere.

# PRECIOUS WORD
October 24, 2007

I wrap Your Word in silver
    then wrap it again in gold,
I place it in my mind
    where it never grows old.

It overflows into my life
    and guides my every step,
For it comes from deep within my heart
    that loves You so, where all of it is kept.

In the darkness of the night
    Your praise is on my lips
As I wrap my mind around You,
    in a state of sacred bliss.

Our spirits are united
    on a level high above,
There where I feel Your Presence,
    I'm embraced by Your sure love.

I begin to thank You for
    Your blessings great and small,
Then suddenly I realize
    I could never thank You enough for them all.

## PRAYING FOR THE UNSAVED
### November 16 and 26, 2007

How sad to think of loved ones going to the grave,
    who have not accepted Jesus
In order to be saved.
    let's be conscious of this every day, let's pray.

Why can't they see what God has done,
    through Jesus on the Cross?
Accepting what He did for us,
    was gain for us, not loss.

They'll never hear the angels
    praise Him and rejoice,
Or forever be with loved ones,
    who made Jesus their eternal choice.

# ETERNAL WORDS
January 4, 6, 2008


Your Word in the Bible
    through the pages of Scripture,
Comforts and soothes us
    like a sweet elixir.

Planned redemption,
    true salvation
Leap off the pages
    in sweet jubilation!

Love and forgiveness,
    mercies galore,
All our sins against You,
    our relationship restored!

Your love is endless,
    Your justice is fair,
You discipline us when needed,
    because You care.

## SO GRATEFUL
October 8, 2007

Ever grateful
  ever full of praise,
For all Your many blessings,
  and all Your sweet, sweet ways.

# WISE ADORNMENT
### January 7, 2008

You could have made me different, perfect in beauty, shape, and form,
    but the love of the Father, the Son, and the Holy Spirit
That dwells within me and my love for You, sweet Jesus
    is how I am adorned.

You could have made me smarter
    a genius with a high I.Q.
Instead you filled me
    with the wisdom of You.

I treasure more the wisdom
    than the high I.Q.
As You show me all
    the amazing things that You do.

I would not trade all the intelligence of this world
    for what You've revealed to me,
This human brain will not accompany me
    when I pass into eternity.

Why would I need worldly intelligence
    when I'll have the perfect mind of Christ?
A treasure He paid for willingly
    with His suffering earthly life.

# THE SONG
## March 13, 2008

You are the music in the song
    You are the rhythm and the rhyme.
The opera and the aria,
    You are the Song Divine.

The notes are crystal clear
    Your Word so true and dear
Such harmony and melody
    I preciously keep near.

The music and the notes,
    the rhythm and the rhyme,
You are the songs that sing
    of Your love divine.

# CARRYING YOUR CROSS
### May 17, 2008

I carry Your cross inside me
    and suffer for Your pain,
I lay down my sins before You
    that You washed away like rain.

In the sacredness of Your Presence,
    all I can feel is humble.
Whether I perfectly follow You,
    or whether I should stumble.

Terry Billetter

# THE WAY TO THE CROSS
## Holy Thursday, March 20, 2008

*The Lord gave me this poem three days after my youngest daughter accepted Christ during Holy Week!*

Via Dolorosa –
    the way to the Cross
Where Jesus suffered
    to redeem our loss.

Tears of sadness fill my eyes
    as I think of what You did,
Dear Lord, for me,
    in Your agony.

On the via Dolorosa that day on Calvary,
    and beatings and the whippings that broke Your skin,
Yet there was nothing they could do to You,
    to mar Your love within.

In Your sacrifice
    You paid the debt we owed,
On that old rugged cross,
    with Your pain and with Your blood.

Your mother watched in horror,
    as the sadness pierced her heart,
Although she knew God's plan for You,
    time for the Son of God to carry out His part.

I've thought what if it were my own son
    hanging there in mid-air,
It makes me cry, tears me apart
    to think of him suffering up there.

But my son is not the Creator
    and Divine God of all that is,
He's not pure, perfect, and sinless,
    like my Lord Jesus, who is his.

# MASTER DESIGNER
## June 7, 2008

*I was inspired to write this after watching a series on a Christian channel showing that scientists now agree with the Bible that God created the universe.*

        You are the Creator and Originator
            of the entire universe.
        Your design is the Master Plan, the physics,
            put in place to make it all work.

        There are galaxies and black holes,
            millions of stars and planets out there.
        Who else, but You, could do this?
            who would claim it, or even dare?

        You made this earth so perfectly,
            so we could all survive.
        Too hot, too cold, or out of balance,
            would ensure our human demise.

        Who could create invisible atoms, so tiny
            with neurons, protons, and electrons therein?
        Who else could match Your infinite creativity?
            who else would know how or where to begin?

# CONSTANT PRESENCE
March 1, 2009

Your Presence surrounds me
    inside out – outside in
Up and down – all around
    deep within.

This is where I want to be.
    Your Spirit hovering over me.
In the darkness, silence too, where I experience You,
    this is where I want to be with You.

I'm captivated by Your Word
    whether written or whether heard.
Obliterating all upsetting thoughts
    that attempt to disturb.

# JUMPING FOR JOY
## March 26, 2009

I jump for joy at the sound of Your Word
    it penetrates me, motivates me
To the love You so deserve.

Your Word is always ready in everything I do,
    what's spelled out on the printed page
Consistently proves faithful and true.

You are the Word, the Word is You,
    its power always prevails.
No force can come against it, no force can it derail.

# NEVER FORGET
Good Friday, April 10, 2009

Never forget what He did for you,
    what He suffered on the Cross.
Never forget what He did for you,
    so your salvation would not be lost.

Never forget what His great love must be
    that we cannot conceive,
Our precious Savior's long-suffering
    we only need to receive.

We can't even begin to imagine
    as He hung there on that Cross.
For if He didn't drink from that cup of sorrow,
    He knew our souls would be lost.

# WORSHIP AND PRAISE
June 10, 2008

    I give You my worship.
        I give You my praise.
    Today – tomorrow
        and all of my days.

    I honor and revere You,
        and bow down before You.
    In Your Holy Presence
        is where I adore You.

    My spirit is calm
        and peaceful with Thee
    Blissful, content,
        and in pure ecstasy.

# DEEP LOVE
### July 30, 2008

I love You with a love so deep
    You fill my every cell.
The Father, Son, and Holy Spirit,
    within me live and dwell.

When I accepted Jesus as My
    Lord and Savior,
We came to share an intimacy
    that since then I have savored.

I am guided by the Holy Spirit,
    He teaches me to discern
What decisions to make, what paths to take;
    I need not be concerned.

They will always love me
    beyond measure, beyond comprehension,
Regardless of what realm They are in
    regardless of what dimension.

# CAPTIVATED
### March 1, 2009

I'm captivated by Your Word, Lord,
    whether written or whether heard.
Obliterating all upsetting thoughts
    that try to disturb.

Anxieties and worries simply have no power
    when they come up against the
Sword of the Spirit – no matter what the hour
    they quickly deflate, and dissipate.

Speak His Word with boldness
    as you come before His throne
Remind Him of His promises
    and that He'd never leave you alone.

His Words will give you comfort and
    the weapons that you'll need
To fight whatever fight you're fighting,
    victory for you to succeed!

## NO DOUBT
### October 6, 2009 – A.M.

*Inspired by the book* Who Moved the Stone *by Frank Morison, former atheist. He set out to disprove Jesus' resurrection, but the more he researched the Gospels, the more proof he found that Jesus' resurrection is true.*

Nobody can disprove You, Jesus,
    the truth of what You have done.
You are truth in Word and Deed
    and neither can be undone.

Though doubters may try to
    disprove the facts
They are compelled to reveal
    the truth of Your acts.

The deeper they dig
    and the longer they study
They soon discover
    their disbelief is muddied.

For His truth shines bright
    over the darkness of doubt,
And they end up proclaiming
    Him Lord with a shout!

## YOU IN EVERYTHING
### April 3, 2009 – January 21, 2010

Lord, You are the lovely symphony
    that plays on through my mind
The warmth of the summer sun, and beautiful flowers
    in springtime that bloom, one by one.

I see You in the grapes in the vineyard,
    fragrant, plump, and ripe
And in the pale, full, silvery moon
    that lights up the black of night.

How awesome is Your presence
    in the silence of my days,
Whether in thought or in Your Word
    or with my own voice in praise.

# MY PRECIOUS HOLY SPIRIT
July 9, 2009

You go down to my tears inside
    where Your presence always abides.
Where I feel Your love for me,
    or is it my love for You?

Or rather meshed together,
    I cannot separate the two.
I cannot speak, I can only feel
    this moment.

## GOD ALWAYS KEEPS HIS WORD
October 14, 2009 A.M.

How dare they say
    God's Word is not true
When He always did
    what He said He would do.

So we can believe that
    what He says He will do,
Without doubt or concern
    His Word always comes through.

# HUMILITY
### October 14, 2009 A.M.

When I think of Your love
    and the tears start to flow,
I feel more humility
    than anyone, but You, will ever know.

The suffering and humiliation
    You endured for me,
Unthinkable, incomprehensible,
    As You hung on a tree.

Who loves the sinner as much
    as the Christ?
Willing to suffer as He did
    and give up His life?

# SEARCHING FOR HAPPINESS
### August 10, 2009

*I was inspired to write this poem as I cried while reading about a man who murdered several people in an office because he couldn't find happiness.*

Some people search for happiness
    in all the worldly things
Instead of seeking God
    for all the joy He brings.

The pleasures of the world
    are temporary and brief,
When seeking God, the Holy Father,
    promises everlasting peace.

Evil takes advantage when you stay away from the Word
    the Bible that you didn't read,
The church you don't attend and
    the sermons unheard.

Keeping you away from the God
    who loves you so much,
You deprive yourself of knowing Him
    when you do not stay in touch.

# THE WISDOM OF THE LORD
June 16, 2009

You are a magnificent, holy and sacred
    God whom I adore.
And with each passing day,
    I grow to love You more.

There is so much to learn about You
    revealed in Your Word,
Layer upon layer of wisdom,
    to think that I could learn it all is foolish and absurd.

This life is just the groundwork for Eternity 101,
    delve into His Word
And live it,
    for the best is yet to come!

# WHY TAKE CHRIST OUT OF CHRISTMAS?
### December 24, 2007

Why take Christ out of Christmas?
    isn't that why we celebrate the day?
It is to celebrate His birthday
    and to honor Him this way.

Why celebrate Christmas
    when you don't believe in Christ?
Don't give gifts, decorate a tree, or make all the preparations
    if you don't accept His price.

Why do you find it necessary
    to attack Our Precious Savior
When He has done nothing to you—
    but come to be born on earth to save you?

# THE PACKAGE
## April 2002

The outside is just the wrapping,
    it is the inside that really counts.
It matters not that we are wrapped
    in beautiful bows and ribbons or mere string tied about.

The wrapper does not matter,
    nor the bow with which it's tied,
What matters lies deep within our hearts
    and what goes on inside.

The wrapper fades away with time,
    the ribbons will get torn,
But our spirit that lies beneath it
    will burn bright with the light of the Lord.

In this life the wrapping will wrinkle
    and the bow will bend out of shape.
But it's what is in the package, perfect and whole
    that will walk by the side of Jesus through the heavenly gate.

When the wrapper is removed and the bow is untied,
    and we are presented before God on the throne,
Our souls will be seen as they gleam and they shine
    and God will proclaim, "You are Mine!"

## YOUR PRESENCE IN EVERYTHING
July 19, 2002

I see You in a baby's face, in skies so blue and fair,
    in a lover's sweet and warm embrace.
You are there.
    You're in everything around me everywhere.

You are in the touch of a loving hand,
    a smile of a friend who cares.
How can anyone doubt
    That You are there?

Hearing music, words and song
    singing praises to You loud and strong.
Lifting us up when we are down, or happy in a joyful sound,
    because You are always around.

## EVENING
February 27, 1999

Deep purple shadows at evening befall
    mountains majestic so high and so tall,
Clouded and misty, mysterious too
    showing Your power, quiet and true.

Here down below
    I look up at Your face
And then You surround me
    with Your peace and grace.

## GOD'S WORD

Always fresh
    always new
Never changing
    ever true.

## ALWAYS THERE
July 8, 2002

The beautiful sunsets
    the lakes and the streams,
The fresh smell of grass
    a lazy day's dream.

In a fragrant rosebud
    every petal and leaf
You share in our joys
    and cry with our grief.

You are high in the mountains
    in deep, craggy cliffs,
In the wind in the desert
    blowing sand mounds and drifts.

The wash of the ocean
    on sun-drenched shore
Makes me feel the connection
    I once knew before.

We see You in autumn
    in vibrant maples and oaks
And the smell of fires
    and wood-burning smoke.

Though summer is over
    there's a chill in the air,
It is time to be still
    and know You are still there.

In the forest of the redwoods
    it's Your silence that I hear,
I am struck with utter speechlessness
    here Your love is so clear.

It reminds me of Your presence
    always constant, still the same.
Through all our years of living
    through the joys and through the pain.

Though the signs of winter
    are not far away
You are still by our side
    every night, every day.

In the chill of winter
    and cold, blustery days
I will ever be thankful and
    give Him my praise.

When the earth is snow-covered
    and the nights cold and long
We have Jesus in Christmas
    giving us hope to go on.

When spring returns
    and the birds start to sing
The flowers burst with color and
    a new song He will bring.

# ARTISTRY IN PERFECTION
### December 18, 2009

How masterful is Your paintbrush
    how beautiful Your design.
The colors in Your palette come only
    from Your mind.

From the stark, white of winter
    to the black silence of the night,
Your artistry is everywhere
    in sparkling angles of light.

Your beauty is ever on display
    in endless hues and shadows
Spread out in the white and bright
    of the cold winter snow blanketing sprawling meadows.

And with the warmth of summer
    comes the vibrant colors of flowers
While they grow and bloom and put on their show
    displaying Your masterful power.

How masterful is Your paintbrush
    how beautiful Your design
With just Your spoken word,
    flowing from Your mind.

# HOLY FATHER
## January 26, 1999

You come to me in quiet
    like soft pastels,
You ride the sea foam
    in a golden crest that of Your Presence tells.

You warm my skin
    through sunlit rays
And feast my eyes
    on sunset skies.

You twinkle on the ocean's ripples
    that dance about the sea.
You're in the sand between my toes
    that surrounds me.

You are the peace high up in the mountains' mist
    creviced in the purple blue,
I am Your child, You are my God
    here it is, just me and You.

# FATHER
August 10, 1999

*The Lord gave me this poem less than one month before my husband's death.*

Father, You are my heart's desire
    You're with me, come what may.
You walk with me through the fires
    keeping me safe all the way.

You calm my fears and give me hope
    when there is none around.
You stay with me when I am down
    and bring me back to solid ground.

When I'm alone
    and want to cry
You enfold me in Your grace—
    far away from this lonely place.

You hold me when I'm weak and down,
    as I listen to your silent sound.
Today, tomorrow – all the same,
    for in You I will always remain.

# TIME
October 10, 2007

I do not care that the days pass quickly,
    or when I see my gray hair distinctly.
When I see my body aging,
    I'm not the least concerned.

These things are just the physical signs
    Inevitable with the passing of time.
Closer is the time for Jesus' return,
    the time for which I yearn.

Jesus will replace my old, worn-out body
    with a new one, radiant and young.
One that will live with Him forever,
    because of the Cross on which He hung.

I do not care that the days pass quickly,
    nor when the dawn fades into dusk.
One day less I have to fight the fight,
    that much closer to God's holy presence—my delight.

# TRAVELING UP
### January 15, 2004

Don't be sad when I leave you,
    don't be sad when I'm gone,
Grieve for just a little while,
    but don't let it last too long.

Life—the words of God's beautifully written song
    and now I've gone to be with Him
In His melody, joined where the words
    and the song belong.

# WAITING FOR JESUS
February 10, 2010

How many more tears must we cry, dear Lord
    before you return to this earth?
How much more must we suffer, Lord,
    before our final rebirth?

We anticipate Your coming,
    with hope and trust and faith,
Looking forward to the Rapture,
    when we can celebrate!

Our tears dried up, our suffering erased
    as we join with the angels and
All the saints in heaven,
    praising Your love and grace.

# DEDICATION

Lord, I dedicate my house to You
    every nook and every cranny,
Every nail and every screw.
    I am only able to live here, because of what You do.

The floor and roof
    the walls within
All make me smile
    for in here You live.

You have blessed me so abundantly,
    that I can hardly take it in.
Your presence here I so enjoy,
    It's where I feel Your peace and joy.

I talk to You throughout the day
    about my thoughts and concerns.
And I pray for family and friends
    listening for what I might learn.

For in You I find my shelter
    like a baby bird in its mother's nest.
In You I feel the contentment
    of Your sweet and loving rest.

# THOUGHTS AND EMOTIONS

When I think of You and all Your creation,
    my soaring thoughts travel beyond elation,
Then tears of appreciation fill my eyes,
    as I look up to the beautiful blue sky.

It's not a temporary emotion,
    this love I feel for You.
It penetrates my every fiber
    for all that in me You do.

It makes me want to be perfect,
    but I know that cannot be,
For the Only One who is perfection
    is Your beautiful, blessed Son.

As I read Your Word and study,
    I am thrilled to my very core,
Realizing how much You love me,
    I am humbled and I am in awe.

# LOSS OF A CHILD

Sweet baby, tender child
    blessed their lives for a little while.
Taken by God with love
    surrounded and escorted by the angels above.

Free from pain, free from harm,
    embraced by the Father's loving arms.
He will live and grow with never a care,
    until the day you join him there.

Time is only temporary, the present is only a pause,
    when you live in eternity you will then understand the cause.
He'll live and learn and love and grow
    in Jesus' love – this I know.

# THE BEST THAT THERE IS
### February 12, 2005

*My inspiration for this poem came as I was reflecting on how very exciting and special my dad made Christmas mornings for my brother and me. We were convinced by the sounds he made that Santa's reindeer were prancing on the roof as they were leaving; the Christmas carols playing on the radio and the beautifully decorated tree made everything magical! Even at my young age, the manger scene was very special and I had the privilege of inserting the bulb inside to light it. I still love setting up the manger with each passing year as I contemplate Christ's birth.*

The best that is here
    is not the best that there is,
There is so much more
    that He has in store.

The secrets are the Lord's
    that He does not reveal,
He plans to use the element of surprise
    so that His joy we do not steal.

Like the father on Christmas morning,
    knowing what the presents contain,
Happiness lights his children's faces
    after which a glow remains.

As we live in Jesus,
    basking in Christ's peace,
He'll gradually reveal those mysteries
    in which we have been asleep.

We can't begin to imagine
    our joy and peace with Him,
The beauty of His heaven
    and all that is therein.

That's why He doesn't tell us,
    we just could not comprehend,
The light, the joy, the happiness
    that will meet us at the end.

# GOD'S SENSITIVITY
February 6, 2006

Your sensitivity is like a flower
    that opens gently in the spring.
It flows over and out of You
    and onto every good thing.

It can show Itself outwardly
    with deep feeling and care,
Or can fold up in self-protectiveness
    so Itself it does not bare.

It stems from the love
    that You possess
Positioned in a deep, abiding
    and loving rest.

# OVERFLOWING
### February 1, 2005

You fill my soul to overflowing,
    my love has no where else to go.
You overflow it spreading outward
    ever-reaching all I know.

Rippling gently here
    and rippling outward there,
Flowing far and wide,
    everywhere.

May Your love always touch
    the ones for which I care,
So they too can spread
    Your love everywhere.

# THE LIGHT OF JESUS
## May 8, 2003

There are no cloudy days in Heaven
    no days of dark and gloom.
But everlasting sunshine
    in the absence of the moon.

If we look within our hearts
    we will find the sunshine there,
For it is tucked in Jesus' Presence
    who is residing there.

Though the skies are ever-changing
    and turn from blue to gray,
Jesus is the Constant
    who is with you every day.

## SMALL AND BIG
### February 2, 2007

We are very small yet very big
    You ask, how can that be?
It is because He who lives within us
    is the Holy Trinity.

Our strength comes not from flesh and bone
    it's from our faith within,
Inside us lives God's love and mercy
    He is the power that lies therein.

Beyond our comprehension
    is a God we cannot conceive,
But all He really yearns for
    is His love for us to receive.

# SACRED PLACE
### February 6, 2007

I know this is one of those moments
    when tears fall down my face.
I know this is a special time
    when I'm in Your sacred place.

I cannot explain why tears are falling,
    I can feel You all around.
All I know is that it is so beautiful,
    here on holy ground.

I feel Your presence within me,
    I never feel alone.
Your Spirit fills me up
    down to the marrow of my bone.

Inside me You have made Your home
    Your silent Presence lives there,
To guide and comfort me
    When my soul to You I bare.

I'm amazed that You want to be so close
    so I can talk to You every day,
How rich and blessed I am to know
    that You are only a thought away.

Private and personal together
    we are wrapped in Your beauty and love,
A precious gift given to me this morning
    You gave me from above.

How lovely and gentle is Your presence
    so pure, so sweet and true.
If only unbelievers knew,
    they would never, ever turn away from You.

## YOU ARE THE ONE

*This poem was my entry for the Valentine's Day Contest that appeared in the* Times-News *Newspaper, in Twin Falls, Idaho, February 10, 2002. Although it was not the winning entry, it was the first to appear among the twenty-five best of the rest.*

When I first met you, I never thought
    you'd be the one, but as we got to know each other
Midst the laughter and the fun,
    I knew you were the one.

Eventually we married
    in later years you were ill,
Our love grew stronger
    As your health went downhill.

We grew in our faith
    through struggles and strife
As God showed us how to live
    downhill with your life.

God's love always there
    through the darkest of times
As your life ebbed away
    in total decline.

As I think of you now
    and the love that we shared,
Wherever you are
    you know we still care.

Never thought you'd be the one
   I would love after the fun
Who I would love until your
   life was done.

*-In loving memory of my husband, Dale*
* - July 8, 1932 – October 1, 1999*

# LIFE'S TREASURES
## March 2002

Treasure your family and friends
    tell them you love them each day
For you never know the time
    when they will be taken away.

For life is so precious
    hanging in a fragile balance.
Think twice before you lash out in anger
    or spew out words of malice.

We are capable of loving
    only because God loved us first
He planted that inside us
    for which we will forever thirst.

The lesson to be learned here
    is that the more you give in love
The more it pleases God
    as He blesses you with His love.

When life's journey is over
    know it is not the end
For there is no separation
    when God is your Best Friend.

# DEAR GOD

I want You in my life all of the time
    blending the parts until they are fine
Letting me feel Your comfort and strength
    in full force which pours out in my confidence.

In You everything is about perfection
    as you work with our weaknesses to create correction.
You mold the clay, You bend the vine
    until, through Jesus, in Your eyes we become divine.

You lead us here and guide us there
    we are always in Your loving care.
Can I ever thank You enough for the blessings You show?
    it is simply impossible for me to know.

## CHANGING GEARS

Time to change gears
    and go forward in life,
To leave my struggle
    with grief and strife.

To go in reverse only
    worsens the hurt
As the memories return
    to my mind in spurts.

But the Lord is my Keeper
    moving the gears
Positioned to go forward
    through my remaining years.

# GROWING OLD

Let's grow old together, Lord
    with You by my side
To comfort, lead, and love me
    with You as my guide.

When I come to You in troubles
    there You open up my eyes
Where You show me Your presence
    amidst the gray and troubling skies.

## GOD'S CREATION

The pure, white clouds that float against
    a clear cerulean sky
The trees and rocks and forests
    that please the naked eye.

Lord, You made all the calculations
    for the people the earth could hold
For the present and the future
    back in ancient days of old.

# THANK YOU!
## November 1999

Thank You and thank You and thank You again
    my thanks will flow till the Earth sees its end.
I'll continue in Heaven to glorify You and share with my loved ones
    who already know all the beautiful, caring things that You do.

My love for You always makes me cry,
    when I think of how Jesus, Your blessed Son, died.
My beautiful Jesus was spat on and mocked
    but He endured it to save the Good Shepherd's flock.

It grieves me to think of His suffering and pain
    this He did for you and for me, and our eternal gain.
So let's thank Him and thank Him and thank Him each day
    for this priceless gift we can never repay.

When we see Him in Heaven and
    look up in His face
He will see in our hearts
    all the thanks for His grace.

# IN LOVE
### September 10, 2009

I fall in love with You all over again
    each and every day
Your love and never-failing kindness
    is present as You guide me in Your way.

Your Presence surrounds and excites me
    so sweet and so pure,
As it dances all around me
    while my thoughts of You endure.

# FACE TO FACE
### December 2002

When I see You face to face
    in Your radiant, glowing grace
Will you let me touch Your face
    to embrace You?

To gently touch each wound
    You suffered on the Cross
So eternity would be our gain
    and not our loss.

My tears of sadness brush Your skin
    for the heartache that I feel within
Each time I think of how You died
    for all my sins.

I'm so embarrassed and ashamed
    that my sins caused You all this pain.
The way that You love me
    knowing You were not to blame.

Your love reaches down to the innermost
    depth of my soul
And the way in which You guide the love
    working in me to make me whole.

Your love for me is endless
    You show it in Your care,
It reaches to my very core
    opening up my soul to bare.

I'm not ashamed to cry for You
    for everything You do.
I only wish the tears I shed
    could wipe away the agony You went through.

You are the life that never ages
    pulsing deep within my soul,
The flame that feeds the fire
    through all my years of old.

Your Holy Spirit lives as One with mine
    destined to one day transcend this earthly time.
When I will leave all troubles and sadness behind
    to be with You, my dear, sweet Jesus divine!

# COME TO MY TABLE
## July 4, 2004

Will You come to my table?
    please sit down with me
Will you share this dinner
    which I prepared for You joyfully?

I'd be honored to have You
    sitting here next to me
So in Your presence I could honor
    and give praise to Thee.

I'd tell you how thankful
    I am for Your blessings,
And the way during sad times
    Your love has caressed me.

I wonder what exactly
    You would say
I really don't know,
    doesn't matter anyway.

I do know Your Words
    would be gentle, sweet, and kind
Full of compassion,
    and love that knows no end in time.

Would You talk about
    Abraham, Moses, and the prophets of old?
Or tell of the prophecies
    already foretold?

Or Your return to this world
    to make everything right?
To bring peace and love
    and stop all the fights?

I'd just love to sit next to You
    and gaze into Your eyes
To see Your love and kindness
    in the God who is all wise.

# TO MY FRIENDS AT BIBLE STUDY
May 3, 2003

Your sweet and shining faces
    mirror the beauty of your souls,
Compassion fills your hearts
    ever caring – ever bold.

Each of you is special
    God has blessed you in His own way,
I can see it in your faces
    as we together speak our say.

It's been a privilege and an honor
    to share your thoughts in class,
They will be long remembered
    and will forever last.

I cannot read this poem
    without tear-filled eyes,
For the feelings that will surface
    are impossible to hide.

Now that the year is over
    and we go about our way,
May God's blessings follow you
    as you stroll through summer's days.

It is my prayer when we're back in class
    that I will find some of you there,
To learn even more of our dear, sweet Lord
    and the many more lessons we'll share.

# HIGHEST EDUCATION
December 21, 2009

No higher education necessary
    no diplomas or credentials
The Holy Spirit will give you all you need
    to be used by Him
He'll give you all the essentials.

His gifts cannot only be found in a college or school
    but through His infinite wisdom
As He works through you
    to do His work by serving Him
And bringing souls into His kingdom.

# LORD JESUS

He didn't have comfort
    He owned not a thing,
He came as a man
    but is really a King!

Had no bed of His own
    to lay His head on,
At the end of the day
    in a place He could call home.

Many times He was lonely
    seeking solitude with God
For comfort and guidance
    in the steps He would trod.

He spoke only what the Father told Him
    never uttering a word of His own
When teaching His Word in the temple,
    giving honor to God on the throne.

# DESPAIR AND PRAYER
### December 18, 2009

*This poem was given to me while I was sick. I believe it was the Holy Spirit reassuring me He was with me while I prayed for healing.*

As I lay there in sickness
    during my time of despair
I prayed to the Lord
    and He answered my prayer.

I didn't let doubt interfere with my hope
    for I knew the power of the words that I spoke.
From Scripture they came with their promise of healing,
    I believed – accepted, and saw what they were revealing.

They overcame the despair
    residing in the flesh,
As the victory of the Spirit took over
    to give me rest.

# THE LORD'S GRIEF
### February 3, 2007

Do you cry, Lord?
    for the sadness of humankind?
For the sickness people suffer?
    their disobedience has maligned?

Lord, how deep Your grief must be
    when you see humanity
Walk away and
    turn away from Thee.

Did you cry?
    when You watched Your Son die on a tree?
When He shed His blood
    for all humanity?

## NO GOING BACK
October 4, 2007

You cannot go back and do it over
    you cannot undo what's been done
But you can ask for your forgiveness
    for which God gave His Son.

It does not matter where you have been
    what you did or did not do.
It only matters what God has done
    in His love, He's forgiven you.

## SEEING YOU
### February 2, 2010

Lord, may they see You in my eyes
    may they hear You in my voice
When I speak.

May they see You in my actions, Lord,
    in all that I do,
And may it be You they desire to seek.

## SEEDS
January 26, 2010

*The inspiration for this poem came to me while glancing at a newspaper ad: "8/$1 garden seeds" at a local hardware store.*

Now is the time to start thinking
    of the seeds we will plant in the spring.
To benefit from the harvest
    that the summer and fall will bring.

But I ask you, what seeds of God's Word
    are you planting in your heart
So the fruit they'll produce
    will have a good start?

You'll not know now
    what God's harvest will bring,
But you will know that He'll use it
    for every good thing.

# EVERYTHING OF BEAUTY

In everything of beauty that's Him in them,
    He's there—He's in the wind – the cool and starry night
The mountains and the azure sea
    and He is always there inside of you and me.

He is the beauty of the rose so colorful and sweet,
    when your face comes near its fragrance
It is Him that you will greet.
    Who else could make them smell so sweet, do you suppose?

When you are kind to someone
    He has made His presence clear
And when you need a friend for comfort
    He, again, is near.

## ALL YOU EVER WANTED

You created us and loved us as we are Your very own,
    before we were born, we were with You at home.
Your love transcends all we are able to think,
    as we try to no avail, only to dead-end at our mind's brink.

You're above all there is – powerful beyond imagination,
    the world, stars, and skies – entire universes Your creation.
You blew into dust to create man,
    for loneliness was an unwanted part of Your plan.

From the very beginning You loved us,
    just how much is impossible to perceive.
All You ever wanted was for us to love You,
    and Your love to receive.

Your gift was Your Son to show how much You care,
    through Him You showed us You are kind and You are fair.
You are just and true in all that You do,
    we need only to place our trust in You.

You are faithful and gracious,
    understanding and kind.
And the Good Book
    describes You – everlasting—for all time.

You are all things to each of us,
    what we need You to be.
Whatever the circumstances,
    Your ways are always perfect, this I see.

# THE PROPHETS
July 13, 2009 and August 3, 2009

Present-day prophets
    and prophets of old
Give us Your message
    the way that it's told.

Warnings and visions
    of things yet to come
Promising guidance
    by The Holy One.

Be not of this world—
    be true to your faith—
And you will endure because of His grace
    so you can endure to finish the race.

## QUIETLY BEAUTIFUL
January 16, 2000


Quietly beautiful, all of my life,
    during life's many trials and strife.
You're here in the dark, You're here at dawn,
    You're the musical notes, of my everyday song.

I think of You in comfort,
    I call on You in pain.
You're like raindrops on the flowers
    who thirst for the spring rain.

Dark night, starry night
    pale moon shining silvery white.
Dawn's arising lights the way
    for my Saviour to be with me today.

# YOUR POETRY, LORD
April 22, 2001


In silence and in darkness
    in the still of the night
You give me gifts of poetry
    in which my soul delights.

They reach the depth of my being and open up all my feelings,
    it makes me want to tell the whole world
Of Your sweet, perfect love
    that will be revealed to us when You bring us home to love.

You're the excitement of first love,
    the happiness of wedded bliss,
The joy of a newborn baby and the tenderness of a kiss
    and of every person's lovely wish.

You're the eagerness of anticipation
    before every happy occasion.
The element of surprise
    in every celebration.

But what most of us do not know
    is that You are so much more.
You are saving the best for last
    by giving us forevermore!

# WHEN IT'S OVER
### October 2000

There's no place to go when it's over
    there's no place to run and hide.
When the music is done, it's the end of the road
    it's the very last ride.

All the chances you were given
    during life have now run out.
You've completed your life's journey
    now you'll find out if you've won the bout.

When you see His face, will He take your hand
    will He walk with you to the Promised Land?
Or will His face be sad and His voice be low
    as He says, "I'm sorry, you cannot go."

He placed His love within your heart
    but there it died without a spark.
He knew the price you'd have to pay
    if you turned away… and did you turn away?

# MIRACLE NIGHT
## January 30, 2003

*This is about a terrible night in the hospital when the doctor told me my husband would not make it through the night. He was almost dead and unresponsive. The Lord gave me this poem about five or six years after his passing.*

I called to You as a child that night
    in darkness and despair.
The night was cold and lonely
    but Your Presence filled the air.

His life was hanging on a thread
    ready to expire,
But through my faith and hope in You,
    my spirit was raised higher.

Your comfort came in Scripture Words
    read to me in school as a child.
The hymns of praise circling 'round my head
    kept me hanging on, all the while.

I asked You for his life back, Lord,
    if that would be Your will,
Unaware you were already answering my prayer
    while yet he lay lifeless and still.

As I continued to praise You throughout the night
    and thank You, Lord, for all You had done,
His eyes opened wide and he awoke once again
    Your victory over death had been won.

My eyes filled with tears of thankfulness
    my mouth was filled with Your praise,
As I witnessed Your life-giving miracle,
    he had come back to me from the grave!

## SEASONS – SPRING
### December 8, 2009

As the cool, crisp air begins to spread over the earth
    and the yellow-green leaves start to burst,
God ushers in the new spring season
    as He warms the hard brown earth.

He refreshes us from the cold, harsh winter reflecting
    His hope of a new beginning.
His array of colors and fragrances clean as birds begin chirping
    and mating adding life to His spectacular scene.

It is God's almighty power
    as He presents His fresh new landscape,
Revealing His wonder and beauty
    in ways we cannot escape.

Give praise to our God, our Creator
    who gives us these sights to behold,
It is His gift of natural beauty
    that every spring is gloriously retold.

# REFLECTIONS
October 11, 2009

As I think of the years behind me and
    the trouble You have brought me through,
You were always right there beside me
    helping me do all I needed to do.

My peace and hope always came from Your Word
    where I received comfort in great times of stress.
They never disappointed – consistent and true
    Your advice was always the best!

When I opened the Bible anxious moments disappeared
    as I read verses that dispelled my fears.
I knew I could trust all that You said and
    that they would remove these thoughts of dread.

The words in the Bible overflow like fresh springs
    opening the reader's mind to the revelation it brings.
A constant flow of knowledge poured into the spirit,
    God's kingdom overflowing, its wisdom rings.

Its source inexhaustible,
    its truth so pure,
Opening the path to the supernatural,
    The Good Shepherd at the door.

All who are thirsty
    drink in the Good Word
It will thrill and surprise you
    taking you to levels unheard.

## GOD'S GIFT OF WORDS
### September 1, 2001

You give me so many beautiful poems, Lord,
    so meaningful – so divine.
I know they come from You
    for I don't know how to rhyme.

They flow across my mind
    like a gentle, whispering breeze,
And then and there I write the words
    with a sweet and flowing ease.

The words come to me when
    I'm thinking and praising You,
It's there in the stillness of my mind
    that Your lovely poetry beautifully unwinds.

If I try to write a poem
    nothing comes to mind,
Until I am inspired by You,
    Lord Most Holy and Divine.

# UNCOMMON
May 2, 2008

Anything but common
    with poise and dignity,
You shed Your blood nailed to a tree
    at Calvary, and I am forever free!

My feelings deep,
    my words are few,
I surrender myself
    completely to You.

# INNER LONGING
### December 21, 2009

There is an inner longing
    an emotion I cannot describe;
Maybe it was when I was with You, Lord,
    before the beginning of time.

Although Your Spirit lives in me
    it's not the same as when I was There,
In your total peace and contentment
    minus the grief of this world I bear.

Although You have not yet returned to Earth
    for Your kingdom to rule and reign,
I look forward, ever hopeful, to
    Your peace it will bring again.

For my longing will only be satisfied
    with the sight of You, my King,
When everlasting praises to You
    I will forever sing!

# THREE PRECIOUS SOULS
## September 1, 2001

You blessed me with three little souls
    to bring into this world,
One handsome baby boy
    and two beautiful baby girls.

To care for and protect,
    to teach them right from wrong
And teach them how to love and be kind
    as they grew and matured, while I nurtured them along.

You filled my heart, Lord,
    with an endless love, you see
To love them more and more each day
    with a limitless capacity.

How grateful I am, Father, for these three most precious gifts
    and in this beautiful love, the Holy Spirit lifts
Me humbly before You, all my imperfections You sift
    showing me the essence of Your three most precious gifts.

## ANDREW
December 1999

*I was led by the Holy Spirit through agonizing emotion and many tears to write this poem after hearing that a secretary I knew had given birth, in November, to a beautiful still-born baby boy. The Holy Spirit meant for these words to comfort her and give her hope of seeing her child again. I enclosed it with a Christmas card that I sent her that year.*

He gave you a child, then took him away
    returned him to Heaven where he'll grow and play.
Until the time comes when you meet him there
    years from now with much to share.

The angels will teach him what he should know
    as he spends time in heaven and continues to grow.
Just think of the joy when you meet face to face
    and the peace you will share in God's heavenly place.

You'll know him when again you meet
    without any memory of sorrow or grief.
The light of the Lord will shine on his face and he'll say,
    "Mom, we'll be together always in this beautiful place."

He'll never know sickness, nor heartache or pain
    but will live with The Father—the ultimate gain.
You will then have forever to love, live, and laugh
    while leaving behind what happened in the past.

When your days here are over, you'll understand why
    your time with him was brief and too soon a goodbye.
Then Our Father will lovingly give you the reason
    why He took back your son in his life's early season.

# WALKING WITH THE LORD
February 18, 2010

Come, walk with me, Jesus, along the soft white sand
    You and I together walking hand in hand.
Far out in the distance, I see a cresting wave
    rolling in with the tide, as it rolls up on the land.

Will You talk about Heaven and the things
    I want to know?
Or talk about Abraham, Isaac, and Jacob
    is that where Your conversation will go?

What about the Rapture?
    will You reveal more than Your Word?
Or must I wait for the trumpet blast
    that will at that time be heard?

Will You tell of eternity
    and what it will be like for me?
Or will You tell me softly, be patient, just wait,
    and one day soon you will see?

## PRAISE YOU, LORD
### January 22, 2010

Your words come down from Heaven,
    to settle in my mind,
They come together beautifully
    to form a poem that rhymes.

I don't know why He chooses
    to bless me in this particular way,
Except to say that years ago He gave me
    the gift of praise on that particular day.

It's a gift from The Holy Spirit
    I'm so honored to receive,
For when I am praising Him
    it's Him I know I please.

# SPIRITUAL DIET
January 22, 2010

How is your spiritual diet?
    do you feed it with God's Word?
Is it nourished with God's wisdom?
    or are they Words you've never heard?

The right foods you eat protect you from illness
    to keep you healthy and strong,
But God's Word gives us protection and comfort and
    in it we can never go wrong, it is always where we belong.

Jesus says He is the "bread of life"
    He feeds the hungry spirit.
His living water satisfies and
    quenches the spirit within it—like nothing else.

Your Word is sweeter than honey
    that I take in and apply,
Know that It always speaks truth and healing
    and that It can never lie.

If our spirits are not fed daily
    disconnected from His source
Then we can be led away quickly
    by an unwanted, evil force.

The Word is our only protection, the Word is our only guide,
    the Word is our only assurance
That will lead us to the heavenly side
    where we will one day become His bride!